American Indian Authors

A representative bibliography

Compiled by Arlene B. Hirschfelder

Association on American Indian Affairs, Inc.
432 Park Avenue South, New York, N.Y. 10016

NO Vi

Photograph on cover by Martin J. Dain.

FOREWORD

AMERICAN INDIANS are largely misunderstood because they have been described by non-Indians who all too often fail to grasp the dynamics of Indian cultures and who project their own cultural biases into their works. In addition, the mass communications media continue to contribute greatly to this misunderstanding by depicting American Indians in a stereotyped and derogatory manner.

This bibliography was compiled to inform people about the extensive body of oral and written literature authored by American Indians. In this way, we hope to encourage readers to learn firsthand about historical and contemporary Indian life and thought.

The literary contributions of American Indians often have gone unnoticed because of the peculiar way publishers and bibliographers have listed books authored by Indians. It has long been customary to promote books under the names of the investigators or editors who record or revise material written or narrated by Indians rather than under the names of the people who deserve the primary credit—the Indians.

In order to awaken the public to the literature of American Indians, all works in this bibliography are listed under the names of the Indians who narrated or wrote them.

The bibliography is followed by two supplementary sections. The first section lists a selection of anthologies of American Indian oral and written literature. The second section lists a selection of periodicals published by American Indian tribes and organizations.

3

American Indian Authors Listed by Tribe

Apache
  Geronimo

Arapaho
  Anonymous, Arapaho
  Sweezy, Carl

Assiniboine
  Courchene, Richard
  Dumont, Robert V., Jr.
  Long, James Larpenteur (First Boy)

Bella Bella
  Gladstone, Willy

Blackfeet
  Bad Head
  Buffalo Child Long Lance, Chief
  Welch, James

Cahuilla
  Chief Meyers
  Costo, Rupert

Catawba
  Owl, Mrs. Samson

Cherokee
  Beeler, Joe
  Bronson, Ruth Muscrat
  Henry, Jeannette
  Kilpatrick, Anna Gritts
  Kilpatrick, Jack Frederick
  Oskison, John Milton
  Ridge, John Rollin (Yellow Bird)

Cheyenne
  Anonymous, Cheyenne
  Cohoe, William

Howling Wolf
  Stands in Timber, John
  Wooden Leg

Chippewa
  Copway, Ceorge
    (Kah-ge-ga-gah-bowh)
  LaDuke, Vincent (Sun Bear)
  Vaudrin, Bill

Choctaw
  Wright, Muriel Hazel

Clackamas Chinook
  Howard, Victoria

Coos
  Buchanan, Jim

Crow
  Plenty-Coups
  Two Leggings

Eskimo
  Senungetuk, Joseph
  Willoya, William

Flathead
  McNickle, D'Arcy

Fox
  Anonymous, Fox

Hopi
  Fredericks, Oswald White Bear
  Nequatewa, Edmund
  Qoyawayma, Polingaysi (Elizabeth
    Q. White)
  Sekaquaptewa, Helen
  Talayesva, Don C.

Kalapuya
  Hudson, John

Kashaya
  Herman, James
  Parrish, Essie

Kiowa
  Momaday, Natachee Scott

Kiowa-Apache
  Whitewolf, Jim

Klikitat
  Hunt, Joe

Kwakiutl
  Anonymous, Kwakiutl
  Nowell, Charles James
  Sewid, James

Mohawk
  Deserontyou, John
  Monture, Ethel Brant
  Newell, William B.

Mohawk-Delaware
  Lone Dog, Louise

Navajo
  Bennett, Kay
  Cha-la-pí
  Left Handed
  Mitchell, Emerson Blackhorse
  Morgan, William
  Mr. Moustache
  Old Mexican
  Son of Former Many Beads

Nez Perce
  Chief Joseph
  Phinney, Archie
  Yellow Wolf

Nootka
  Clutesi, George C.

Okanogan
  Hum-ishu-ma (Mourning Dove)

Omaha
  LaFlesche, Francis

Oneida
  Archiquette, Oscar
  Dockstader, Frederick J.

Osage
  Griffis, Joseph K. (Chief Tahan)
  Kimball, Yeffe
  Mathews, John Joseph

Otomi
  Villasenor, David

Paiute
  Hopkins, Sarah Winnemucca
  Lowry, Annie
  Newland, Sam
  Stewart, Jack

Papago
  Chona, Maria

Pawnee
  Murie, James R.

6

American Indian Authors

ALFORD, THOMAS WILDCAT, Shawnee.
Civilization, as told to Florence Drake. Norman:
Univ. of Oklahoma Press, 1936. 203 pp. Illus. Out
of print.

The author, a great-grandson of Tecumseh, discusses Shawnee life and history
and his own schooling and work in Shawnee affairs.

AMERICAN INDIAN HISTORICAL SOCIETY.
*Our Inaccurate Textbooks: The American Indian
Case.* San Francisco: The Indian Historian Press*,
1970. 200 pp. $4.00.

The study evaluates 160 textbooks now in use in both the public schools and the
Bureau of Indian Affairs schools of the United States. The evaluation contains
a comprehensive list of criteria for every subject area being taught in the social
sciences in schools.

ANONYMOUS.
Nevada Indians Speak, ed. by Jack D. Forbes. Reno:
Univ. of Nevada Press, 1967. 293 pp. Illus. $5.75.

A collection of first-person statements dealing with first encounters with white
men and the struggle to maintain an identity despite the influx of a new and domi-
nant culture.

ANONYMOUS, Arapaho.
"Narrative of an Arapaho Woman," ed. by Truman
Michelson. *American Indian Anthropologist* No. 35.
Menasha, Wisc.: American Anthropological Asso-
ciation, 1933. pp. 595-610. Out of print.

This narrative of a seventy-seven-year-old woman, given through an interpreter,
reveals the culture of the Arapaho Tribe during the last half of the nineteenth
century as well as the role of a woman in Arapaho society.

*The Indian Historian Press is a private publishing venture organized by members of the
American Indian Historial Society. Its purpose is to publish books by Indians about the history, culture, and current condition of American Indians.

The press has many titles scheduled for publication during 1970. To secure information on
new titles write: The Indian Historian Press, 1451 Masonic Ave., San Francisco, Calif. 94117.

ANONYMOUS, Cheyenne.
Narrative of a Southern Cheyenne Woman, ed. by
Truman Michelson. Smithsonian Miscellaneous Collections, Vol. 87, No. 5. Washington: Smithsonian
Institution, 1932. 13 pp. Out of print.

A Cheyenne woman of the late nineteenth and early twentieth centuries describes
her marriage and family life, and tribal customs, beliefs, ceremonies, games, etc.

ANONYMOUS, Fox.
The Autobiography of a Fox Woman, ed. by Truman
Michelson. U.S. American Ethnology Bureau Annual Report No. 40. Washington: Government Printing Office, 1925. pp. 291-349. Out of print.

The narrative life story of a Fox woman (whose name is withheld on agreement)
is presented in Fox and English texts. The narrator discusses her life during the
late nineteenth and early twentieth centuries and the customs and beliefs of the
Fox Tribe at that time.

ANONYMOUS, Kwakiutl.
Kwakiutl Tales, ed. by Franz Boas. Columbia Univ.
Contributions to Anthropology, Vol. XXVI. New
York: Columbia Univ. Press, 1935. 230 pp. Out of
print.

Kwakiutl tales narrated by several members of the tribe are presented in Kwakiutl
and English texts (British Columbia).

ANONYMOUS, Sioux.
The Hardin Winter Count, ed. by David Finster.
Museum News, Vol. 26, Nos. 3-4. March-April, 1968.
Vermillion, South Dakota: The Univ. of South
Dakota, 1968. 59 pp. Illus. $1.00 plus postage. Available from Tipi Shop, Inc., P.O. Box 1270, Rapid
City, South Dakota 57701.

A winter count* collected from an unknown member of the Rosebud Sioux Tribe
sometime between 1895 and 1902 by Dr. L. M. Hardin, a physician in the Indian
Service. The count records events for each winter from 1776-1879. Information
on the Sioux Tribe and its relations with other tribes is provided. Interpretations
for each pictograph and comments on each count, drawn from Indian and non-Indian sources, are included.

*Winter count: A picture of the main event each winter. Because the Plains Indians traveled
far on their long hunts and met people from other tribes, they made wider use of pictographs
than did Indians of other regions. Pictographs were also used for messages, warnings, and
treaties, as well as histories.

BAD HEAD, Blackfeet.
A Blackfoot Winter Count, ed. by Hugh A. Dempsey.
Calgary, Alberta: Glenbow Foundation, 1965. 20 pp.
$.75 paperbound. Available from Museum Sales
Desk, Glenbow-Alberta Institute, 902 11th Avenue,
S.W., Calgary 3, Alberta.

Bad Head's winter count is a calendrical and historical record of the years 1810-1883. It provides information on the Blackfeet Tribe and its relations with other tribes. Literal translations for each Blackfeet term, and comments on each count, drawn from a number of sources, are included.

BAD HEART BULL, AMOS, Sioux.
A Pictographic History of the Oglala Sioux, ed. by
Helen H. Blish. Lincoln: Univ. of Nebraska Press,
1967. 562 pp. Illus. by author. $17.95.

Over four hundred drawings and notations done by Bad Heart Bull between 1890 and 1913 are incorporated in this volume to provide a visual record of Sioux culture.

BEELER, JOE, Cherokee.
Cowboys and Indians: Characters in Oil and Bronze.
Norman: Univ. of Oklahoma Press, 1967. 167 pp.
Illus. by author. $7.95.

Reproductions of Beeler's paintings, drawings, and bronzes are accompanied by his explanations of the works.

BENNETT, KAY, Navajo.
Kaibah: Recollections of a Navajo Girlhood. Los
Angeles: Western Lore Press, 1964. 253 pp. Illus.
by author. $7.50.

This autobiographical story of a Navajo girl and her family takes place in New Mexico and covers the years from 1928 to 1935.

BENSON, WILLIAM, Pomo.
"The Stone and Kelsey 'Massacre' on the Shores of
Clear Lake in 1849, the Indian Viewpoint." *California
Historical Society Quarterly,* Vol. XI, No. 3. Sept.,
1932. pp. 266-273. Out of print.

Benson gives an account of the 1849 slaying of two white men in California, basing his description on information gathered from tribal members. His account is not only an historical document, it also provides an insight into Indian psychology in Indian-white relations.

BLACK ELK, Sioux.
*Black Elk Speaks: Being the Life Story of a Holy
Man of the Oglala Sioux,* as told to John G. Neihardt.
Lincoln: Univ. of Nebraska Press, 1961. 281 pp. Illus.
by Standing Bear. $1.50 paperbound.

Originally published in 1932, this is a personal narrative by one of the great
spiritual leaders of the Oglala Sioux. Black Elk, a holy man who was born in
1863, gives a moving account of his life from early boyhood to the massacre at
Wounded Knee in 1890 and the gathering of the Oglala Sioux on the Pine Ridge
Reservation in South Dakota.

BLACK ELK, Sioux.
*The Sacred Pipe: Black Elk's Account of the Seven
Rites of the Oglala Sioux,* ed. by Joseph Epes Brown.
Norman: Univ. of Oklahoma Press, 1953. 144 pp.
Illus. $3.75.

Narrated by Black Elk when he was over ninety years of age, this is an account
of sacred Sioux religious ceremonies.

BLACK HAWK, Sauk.
Black Hawk: An Autobiography, ed. by Donald Jack-
son. Gloucester, Mass.: Peter Smith, 1955. 206 pp.
Illus. $3.75. Also paperbound: Urbana: Univ. of
Illinois Press. $1.75.

In this autobiography, based on an 1833 version, Black Hawk narrates to a government interpreter a seventy-year struggle from his early battles with other tribes
to his last flight from the United States Army.

BRONSON, RUTH MUSKRAT, Cherokee.
Indians Are People Too. New York: Friendship
Press, 1944. 184 pp. Out of print.

In a general discussion of twentieth century Indians, reservation life, Indian values,
family life, education, and leadership are covered.

BUCHANAN, JIM, Coos.
Coos Texts, ed. by Leo J. Frachtenberg. Columbia
Univ. Contributions to Anthropology, Vol. I. New
York: Columbia Univ. Press, 1913. 216 pp. Out of
print.

Coos mythology narrated by Mr. Buchanan is presented in Coos and English
texts (northwest United States).

BUFFALO CHILD LONG LANCE, CHIEF,
Blackfeet.
Long Lance. New York: Cosmopolitan Book Corp.,
1928. 278 pp. Illus. Out of print.

The author describes the experiences of the last tribes to encounter the advancing white man in the Far Northwest (northern Montana, Alberta, Saskatchewan, and British Columbia) during the last quarter of the nineteenth century and the beginning of the twentieth.

BUFFALO CHILD LONG LANCE, CHIEF,
Blackfeet.
*Redman Echoes: Comprising the Writings of Chief
Buffalo Child Long Lance and Biographical Sketches
by His Friends.* Los Angeles: Frank Wiggins Trade
School, Dept. of Printing, 1933. 219 pp. Out of
print.

The author describes the late nineteenth and early twentieth century tribes of the Northwest and western Canada. He includes poetry, and stories about Carlisle, West Point, and tribal customs and ceremonies.

CHA-LA-PÍ, Navajo.
*Navajo Indian Poems: Translation from the Navajo,
and Other Poems,* as told to Hilda Faunce Wetherill.
New York: Vantage Press, 1952. 53 pp. Out of
print.

The poetry recorded here presents the activities of Navajo daily life.

CHIEF EAGLE, D., Sioux.
Winter Count. Denver: Golden Bell Press, 1968.
230 pp. $4.95.

This novel about the Western Sioux in the last quarter of the nineteenth century is primarily a military treatment based on Chief Eagle's interviews with tribal elders.

CHIEF JOSEPH, Nez Perce
"An Indian's View of Indian Affairs." *North Ameri-
can Review,* Vol. CCLXIX, April, 1879. pp. 415-433.
Out of print.

Chief Joseph recounts the events of the 1877 war between his tribe and the United States. He discusses the roles of the U.S. Indian agents and army generals in the hostilities.

CHIEF MEYERS, Cahuilla.
"Chief Meyers" in *The Glory of Their Times: The Story of the Early Days of Baseball Told by the Men Who Played it,* as told to Lawrence S. Ritter. New York: Macmillan Co., 1966. pp.162-176. Illus. $7.95.

Chief Meyers, born in 1880, played baseball for the New York Giants from 1908 through 1915, and was traded to the Brooklyn Dodgers in 1916. In this narrative, Meyers recalls his experiences and acquaintances—Casey Stengel, Chief Bender, and Jim Thorpe among them—in the baseball world.

CHONA, MARIA, Papago.
Autobiography of a Papago Woman, ed. by Ruth Underhill. Menasha, Wisc.: The American Anthropological Association Memoirs, Vol. 46, 1936. 64 pp. Out of print.

Chona, ninety years of age, tells the story of her past, and presents a picture of a Papago woman's role and status in the last quarter of the nineteenth and early twentieth century.

CLUTESI, GEORGE C., Nootka.
Potlatch. Sidney, B.C.: Gray's Publishing Ltd., 1969. Other data unreported.

This is a day-by-day account of a British Columbian Indian winter festival. The ceremony, called a potlatch, is a ritual feast accompanied by lavish gift giving.

COHOE, WILLIAM, Cheyenne.
A Cheyenne Sketchbook, with commentary by E. Adamson Hoebel and Karen Daniels Petersen. Norman: Univ. of Oklahoma Press, 1964. 96 pp. Illus. by author. $5.95.

Cohoe, one of seventy-two warriors from the Great Plains taken as prisoners to Fort Marion, Fla. in 1875, has sketched scenes from his past life and his experiences as a prisoner. These drawings are in three groups: life on the plains, hunting; life on the plains, ceremonies; life at Fort Marion, prisoners of war.

CONFERENCE ON CALIFORNIA INDIAN EDUCATION, California tribes.
Report of the First All-Indian Statewide Conference on California Indian Education. Modesto: California Indian Education Association, Inc., 1967. 88 pp. $2.00 paperbound. Available from publisher, 1349 Crawford Rd., Modesto, Calif. 95350.

This report by an all-Indian committee concerns itself primarily with ways in which the situation of the Indian children in the California school system can be improved.

14

COPWAY, GEORGE
(KAH-GE-GA-GAH-BOWH), Chippewa.
Indian Life and Indian History: By an Indian Author.
Boston: Albert Colby and Co., Inc., 1860. 266 pp.
Out of print.

The author writes about Ojibway (Chippewa) history, culture, and legends to preserve information about the tribe for future generations as well as to help non-Indians understand Indians better.

CORNPLANTER, JESSE J., Seneca.
Legends of the Longhouse. Port Washington, N.Y.:
Ira J. Friedman, Inc., 1963. 218 pp. Illus. by author.
$5.00.

This reprint of a 1938 edition is a collection of the myths and legends of the Seneca Tribe which form the basis of Seneca religion and provide a guide to moral behavior.

COSTO, RUPERT, Cahuilla.
Redman of the Golden West. San Francisco: The
Indian Historian Press, 1970. 184 pp. Illus. $6.25.

This book details the story of American Indians in the region now known as California, Nevada, and Oregon from their origins to the present day.

COURCHENE, RICHARD, Assiniboine-Sioux.
Hell, Love, and Fun. Billings, Mont., 1969. 138 pp.
$1.00 paperbound. Available from Mr. Courchene,
Wolf Point, Montana 59201.

Courchene tells of his military experiences from 1932 to 1944. He writes about the rivalry between the branches of the service, relationships with Australians, and South Pacific natives.

CRASHING THUNDER, Winnebago.
Crashing Thunder: The Autobiography of a Winnebago, ed. by Paul Radin. New York: Dover
Publications, Inc., 1963. 91 pp. $1.00 paperbound.

A republication of a 1920 edition, this life story of a Winnebago man incorporates a great deal of information about the tribe's folklore and customs with a frank treatment of the author's life.

CUERO, DELPHINA, Southern Diegueño.
The Autobiography of Delphina Cuero: A Diegueño Indian, as told to Florence C. Shipek. Los Angeles: Dawson's Book Shop, 1968. 67 pp. $10.00.

In the course of recording the struggle of a displaced Indian in modern society, Mrs. Cuero provides information about the traditional life of California Indians. Food gathering methods, hunting and fishing along the coastal regions, trade relations, leadership selection and role, ceremonial participation, and cultural change are discussed.

DELORIA, ELLA CARA, Sioux.
Dakota Texts. American Ethnological Society Publications, Vol. XIV. New York: G.E. Stechert and Co., 1932. 279 pp. Out of print.

Teton Sioux tales from the Standing Rock (North and South Dakota), Pine Ridge (South Dakota), and Rosebud (South Dakota) Reservations are transcribed in Sioux directly from storytellers who related them to the author. Each tale is accompanied by the author's translation with notes on grammar and customs.

DELORIA, ELLA CARA, Sioux.
Speaking of Indians. New York: Friendship Press, 1944. 163 pp. Out of print.

This is an examination of the most significant elements in the life of a Sioux before white settlement. It discusses the social, religious, economic, and educational adjustments to a new way of life, and the elements of the old way which persist in spite of the encroachments of another culture.

DELORIA, VINE, JR., Sioux.
Custer Died For Your Sins: An Indian Manifesto.
New York: Macmillan, 1969. 279 pp. $5.95.

Mr. Deloria writes of American Indians in today's world. He discusses the roles of treaties, government policies and agencies, the white man's law, missionaries, and anthropologists in contemporary Indian affairs.

DESERONTYOU, JOHN, Mohawk.
A Mohawk Form of Ritual Condolence: 1782, translated by John Napoleon Brinton Hewitt. New York: Museum of American Indian, Heye Foundation, 1928. pp. 87-110. Out of print.

Customary forms of Mohawk sacred rituals and chants are recorded here as they were used in the late eighteenth century.

16

DOCKSTADER, FREDERICK J., Oneida.
The American Indian in Graduate Studies. New
York: Museum of the American Indian, Heye Foun-
dation, 1956. 299 pp. $5.00 paperbound.

Listed here are over 3,500 theses and dissertations from colleges throughout
North America. A supplementary volume is now in progress. The theses deal with
the Indian tribes of North, Central, and South America, and the Eskimos of the
Arctic.

DOCKSTADER, FREDERICK J., Oneida.
*Indian Art in America: The Arts and Crafts of the
North American Indian.* Greenwich, Conn.: New
York Graphic Society, 1966. 224 pp. Illus. $25.00.

North American Indian art is surveyed from its earliest known examples to the
present day.

DOCKSTADER, FREDERICK J., Oneida.
Indian Art in Middle America. Greenwich, Conn.:
New York Graphic Society, 1964. 221 pp. Illus.
$25.00.

Aboriginal art from northern Mexico to southern Panama, including the West
Indies, is surveyed in this volume.

DOCKSTADER, FREDERICK J., Oneida.
*Indian Art in South America: Pre-Columbian and
Contemporary Arts and Crafts.* Greenwich, Conn.:
New York Graphic Society, 1967. 222 pp. Illus.
$27.50.

Here Mr. Dockstader deals with the aboriginal art of South America, up to and
including contemporary cultures.

DOCKSTADER, FREDERICK J., Oneida.
*The Kachina and the White Man: The Influences of
the White Culture on the Hopi Kachina Cult.* Bloom-
field Hills, Mich.: Cranbrook Institute of Science,
Bulletin No. 35, 1954. 204 pp. Illus. by author. Out
of print, but available from the Museum of the
American Indian, New York. $6.00.

This work studies the origins and development of Hopi (and Zuni) ceremonials
and the degree to which they have been changed because of outside cultural
influences.

DOZIER, EDWARD P., Santa Clara Pueblo.
Hano, A Tewa Community in Arizona. New York:
Holt, Rinehart and Winston, 1966. 104 pp. $1.50
paperbound.

Dr. Dozier details the history, development, and present situation of one Indian
community in Arizona.

DOZIER, EDWARD P., Santa Clara Pueblo.
Pueblo Indians of the Southwest. New York: Holt,
Rinehart and Winston, 1970. 192 pp. $3.95 paper-
bound.

An historical and cultural account of approximately twenty Pueblo Indian villages
in the Southwest from their origins to the present—told from the Indian point of
view.

DOZIER, EDWARD P., Santa Clara Pueblo.
"Two Examples of Linguistic Acculturation: The
Yaqui of Sonora and Arizona and the Tewa of New
Mexico," in *Language in Culture and Society,* ed.
by Dell Hymes. New York: Harper and Row, 1964.
pp. 509-520. $14.50.

The adjustments of two Indian languages due to their contacts with other cultures
are treated here.

DUMONT, ROBERT V., JR., Assiniboine.
*Formal Education in an American Indian Com-
munity,* co-authored by Murray L. and Rosalie H.
Wax. Monograph #1, The Study of Social Problems,
Spring, 1964. 126 pp. $3.00. Available from The So-
ciety for the Study of Social Problems, P.O. Box 190,
Kalamazoo, Mich. 49005.

The relationship between an Indian community and its school is traced and docu-
mented through observations made during visits to federal schools. The proposi-
tion that schools serving Indian communities should be controlled by Indians
is treated.

DUMONT, ROBERT V., JR., Assiniboine.
"Learning English and How to be Silent: Studies in
American Indian Classrooms," in *Functions of
Language,* ed. by Dell Hymes and Vera Johns. New
York: Teachers College Press, 1970. Pages and cost
unreported.

General observations of the phenomenon of student silence in Cherokee and
Sioux classrooms. This is a report of field work done in 1967 in Oklahoma and
North Dakota.

EASTMAN, CHARLES ALEXANDER
(OHIYESA), Sioux.
*From the Deep Woods to Civilization: Chapters in
the Autobiography of an Indian.* Boston: Little,
Brown and Co., 1916. 206 pp. Illus. Out of print.

Dr. Eastman tells of his life from his fifteenth year to the second decade of the
twentieth century. His story includes discussion of his college life, medical train-
ing, practice of medicine, and work among Indians.

EASTMAN, CHARLES ALEXANDER
(OHIYESA), Sioux.
Indian Boyhood. New York: McClure, 1904. 289
pp. Illus. Out of print.

Eastman's first book which he describes as "recollections of my wild life,"
pictures the first of three distinct periods in the life of the writer.

EASTMAN, CHARLES ALEXANDER
(OHIYESA), Sioux.
*The Indian Today, the Past and Future of the First
American.* Garden City, N.Y.: Doubleday, 1915.
185 pp. Out of print.

The author discusses the past up to the early twentieth century and makes some
predictions for the future.

EASTMAN, CHARLES ALEXANDER
(OHIYESA), Sioux.
Red Hunters and the Animal People. New York:
Harper and Brothers, 1904. 248 pp. Out of print.

Stories based on the experiences and observations of Sioux hunters are presented
along with fables, songs, and the life-stories of animals according to Sioux legend.

EASTMAN, CHARLES ALEXANDER
(OHIYESA), Sioux.
Soul of an Indian: An Interpretation. Boston:
Houghton-Mifflin, 1911. 170 pp. Out of print.

The author presents religious life as it was before the advent of the white man,
contending that the religion of the Indian is the last thing that a man of another
race will ever understand.

FLYING CLOUD, CHIEF
(FRANCIS BENJAMIN ZAHN), Sioux.
The Crimson Carnage of Wounded Knee. Bottineau,
N. Dak.: Edward A. Milligan, 1967. 12 pp. $1.00
paperbound.

Written for the fiftieth anniversary of Wounded Knee, this is the story of the
massacre as told to the author by White Lance and Dewey Beard, two of the
survivors. Taken down in Sioux and translated into English.

FLYING HAWK, Sioux.
*Firewater and Forked Tongues: A Sioux Chief In-
terprets* U.S. History, as told to M.I. McCreight.
Pasadena, Calif.: Trail's End Publishing Co., Inc.,
1947. Out of print.

Flying Hawk, born about 1852, discusses the history of the United States from
the arrival of the first white man. Included are short narratives about Flying
Hawk himself, Indian philosophy, well-known Indians, and battles between
Indians and non-Indians.

FREDERICKS, OSWALD WHITE BEAR, Hopi.
Book of the Hopi, text by Frank Waters. New York:
The Viking Press, Inc., 1963. 448 pp. Illus. by
author. $10.00. Also paperbound: New York: Ballan-
tine Books. $1.25.

These drawings and source materials provide an account of Hopi historical and
religious world views as interpreted by a Hopi artist in collaboration with a
non-Indian novelist.

GERONIMO, Apache.
Geronimo's Story of His Life, as told to and edited
by Steven Melvil Barrett. New York: Duffield and
Co., 1906. 216 pp. Illus. Out of print.

While Geronimo was imprisoned at Fort Sill, Oklahoma Territory, he dictated
the story of his life, giving both a cultural and an historical account of the
Apaches to Mr. Barrett.

GLADSTONE, WILLY, Bella Bella.
Bella Bella Texts, ed. by Franz Boas. Columbia Univ.
Contributions to Anthropology Vol. V. New York:
Columbia Univ. Press, 1928. 291 pp. Out of print.

Bella Bella tales as narrated by Mr. Gladstone are presented in Bella Bella and
English texts (British Columbia).

GRIFFIS, JOSEPH K. (CHIEF TAHAN), Osage.
Indian Story Circle Stories. Burlington, Vt.: Free
Press Printing Co., 1928. 138 pp. Out of print.

These stories, heard by the author as he grew to manhood, were told by the storytellers of the Kiowa, Cherokee, Choctaw, and Malecite tribes.

GRIFFIS, JOSEPH K. (CHIEF TAHAN), Osage.
Tahan: Out of Savagery into Civilization. New York:
George B. Doran Co., 1915. 263 pp. Out of print.

This autobiography of an Osage, who was born in the middle of the nineteenth
century, covers his varied background as warrior, medicine man, outlaw, scout,
Salvation Army captain, clergyman, and scholar.

HENRY, JEANNETTE, Cherokee.
The American Indian in American History. Indian
Handbook Series #1. San Francisco: The Indian
Historian Press, 1970. 84 pp. $3.00.

This book contains an integrated study of the American Indians throughout
America's national history. The author shows the Indian's role at every stage of
the development of this nation.

HERMAN, JAMES and PARRISH, ESSIE, et al,
Kashaya.
Kashaya Texts, ed. by Robert L. Oswalt. Univ. of
California Publications in Linguistics, Vol. 36.
Berkeley: Univ. of California Press, 1964. 340 pp.
Illus. Out of print.

Traditional stories, myths, tales of the supernatural, and folk history narrated by
the main informants, Parrish and Herman, are recorded and translated in this
collection. Both Kashaya and English texts are given.

HEWITT, JOHN NAPOLEON BRINTON,
Tuscarora.
Articles in the *Handbook of the American Indians
North of Mexico,* ed. by Frederick Webb Hodge.
Scholarly Press, 1968. 2 vols. $75.00.

Hewitt contributed articles to this handbook, originally published in 1912, which
gives brief descriptions of linguistic stocks, confederacies, tribes, tribal divisions,
settlements known to history or tradition, and discusses the origins or derivations
of names, where they are known.

HEWITT, JOHN NAPOLEON BRINTON,
Tuscarora.
"Iroquois Cosmology," in *Bureau of American Ethnology 21st Annual Report*. Washington: Government Printing Office, 1904. pp. 127-339. Illus. Out of print.

Onondaga, Seneca, and Mohawk versions of Iroquois cosmology are given here with original texts and English translations.

HEWITT, JOHN NAPOLEON BRINTON,
Tuscarora.
Journal of Rudolph Friedrich Kurz, ed. by Hewitt, U.S. American Ethnology Bulletin 115. Washington: Government Printing Office, 1937. 382 pp. Out of print.

This account of Kurz' experiences among fur traders and American Indians on the Mississippi and the upper Missouri Rivers covers the years from 1846 to 1852.

HOPKINS, SARAH WINNEMUCCA, Paiute.
Life Among the Piutes: Their Wrongs and Claims, ed. by Mrs. Horace Mann. Boston-New York: G. P. Putnam's Sons, 1883. 268 pp. Out of print.

Mrs. Hopkins, born about 1844, describes her life and her tribe's culture, before and after contact with whites. Her purpose in writing the book was to acquaint the public with the trials her tribe had undergone.

HOWARD, VICTORIA, Clackamas Chinook.
Clackamas Chinook Texts, ed. by Melville Jacobs. Bloomington: Indiana Univ. Research Center in Anthropology, Folklore, and Linguistics, 1958. 2 vols. 292 pp. Out of print.

Songs and oral literature narrated and translated by Mrs. Howard are presented in Clackamas Chinook and English texts (northwest United States).

HOWLING WOLF, Cheyenne.
Howling Wolf: A Cheyenne Warrior's Graphic Interpretation of His People, text by Karen Daniels Petersen. Palo Alto: American West Publishing Co., 1968. 64 pp. Illus. by author. $14.00.

Sketches done by Howling Wolf while being held prisoner at Fort Marion in Florida from 1875 to 1878 tell the story of his people.

HUDSON, JOHN B., Kalapuya.
*Kalapuya Texts: Part I, Santiam Kalapuya Ethno-
logic Texts* and *Part II, Santiam Kalapuya Myth
Texts,* ed. by Melville Jacobs. Univ. of Washington
Publications in Anthropology Vol. XI. Seattle: Univ.
of Washington, 1945. pp. 3-142. Out of print.

Part I. Ninety-two short descriptions of various facets of Kalapuya culture are
narrated and translated by Mr. Hudson. Both Kalapuya and English texts are
provided. Part II. Kalapuya myths, narrated and translated by Mr. Hudson, are
presented in Kalapuya and English texts (northwest United States).

HUM-ISHU-MA (MOURNING DOVE), Okanogan.
*Co-ge-we-a, The Half-Blood: A Depiction of the
Great Montana Cattle Range,* as told to Sho-pow-
tan. Boston: The Four Seas Co., 1927. 302 pp. Out
of print.

This fictional narrative, based on Indian characters from real life, pictures the
closing days of the great cattle range, and the decadence of its reigning head,
the cowboy.

HUM-ISHU-MA (MOURNING DOVE), Okanogan.
Coyote Stories, ed. by Heister Dean Guie Caldwell.
Caldwell, Idaho: Caxton Printers Ltd., 1933. 228
pp. Illus. Out of print.

Hum-ishu-ma relates stories and legends of the Okanogan Indians, a Pacific
Northwest tribe.

HUNT, JOE, Klikitat.
Northwest Sahaptin Texts, ed. by Melville Jacobs.
Univ. of Washington Publications in Anthropology
Vol. II, No. 6. Seattle: Univ. of Washington, 1929.
Illus. 77 pp. $2.50 paperbound.

Thirteen traditional folk tales narrated by Mr. Hunt recall the customs and
mythology of Klikitat culture. Both Klikitat and English texts provided (northwest United States).

HUNTER, LOIS MARIE, Shinnecock.
The Shinnecock Indians. Islip, N.Y.: Buys Brothers,
1952. 90 pp. Out of print.

A descendant of Sachem Nowedonah tells the story of the Shinnecocks before and
after contact with the white man.

KILPATRICK, JACK FREDERICK, and
KILPATRICK, ANNA GRITTS, Cherokee.
*New Echota Letters: Contributions of Samuel A.
Worcester to the Cherokee Phoenix,* ed. by the Kil-
patricks. Dallas: Southern Methodist Univ. Press,
1968. 140 pp. $5.00.

This book contains the letters of a non-Indian missionary, Samuel A. Worcester
—teacher, missionary, and physician to the Cherokee people. The letters reveal
Worcester's personality and his relationships with the Cherokee people and the
editor of the *Cherokee Phoenix,* the newspaper of the tribe in the early nineteenth
century.

KILPATRICK, JACK FREDERICK, and
KILPATRICK, ANNA GRITTS, Cherokee.
*Run Toward the Nightland: Magic of the Oklahoma
Cherokees,* ed. by the Kilpatricks. Dallas: Southern
Methodist Univ. Press, 1967. $5.00.

Medicine and magic rituals, with melodies and words, of the Oklahoma Cherokees
are translated in this volume.

KILPATRICK, JACK FREDERICK and
KILPATRICK, ANNA GRITTS, Cherokee.
*The Shadow of Sequoyah: Social Documents of the
Cherokees. 1862-1964,* trans. and ed. by the Kil-
patricks. Norman: Univ. of Oklahoma Press, 1965.
129 pp. Illus. $4.50.

One hundred years of Cherokee writings covering diverse subjects are represented
in this volume by such primary sources as letters, minutes of meetings, committee
reports, and private memoranda.

KILPATRICK, JACK FREDERICK and
KILPATRICK, ANNA GRITTS, Cherokee.
*Walk in Your Soul: Love Incantations of the Okla-
homa Cherokees,* ed. by the Kilpatricks. Dallas:
Southern Methodist Univ. Press. 1965. 164 pp. $5.00.

These translations from Cherokee are fully annotated as to charms and magic,
and each incantation is accompanied by a discussion of words and images, background, and purpose.

KIMBALL, YEFFE, Osage.
The Art of American Indian Cooking, co-authored by
Jean Anderson. Garden City, N.Y.: Doubleday and
Co., Inc., 1965. 215 pp. Illus. $4.50.

American Indian recipes adapted for today's kitchens include information of foods and food habits of American Indians.

KUNI et al. Walapai.
Walapai Ethnology, ed. by A.L. Kroeber. Memoirs of the American Anthropological Association No. 42. Menasha, Wisc.: American Anthropological Association, 1935. pp. 205-229. Out of print.

Four brief autobiographies reveal the culture of the Walapai in the Southwest during the last quarter of the nineteenth century and the first quarter of the twentieth. Information is included on the facts of the acculturation process as the Walapai see them.

LADUKE, VINCENT (SUN BEAR), Chippewa.
At Home in the Wilderness. Sparks, Nevada: Western Printing and Publishing Co., 1969. Illus. Cost and pages unreported.

This book by a Chippewa discusses survival in the outdoors.

LAFLESCHE, FRANCIS, Omaha.
A Dictionary of the Osage Language. U.S. American Ethnology Bureau Bulletin 109. Washington: Government Printing Office, 1932. 406 pp. Out of print.

An Osage-English dictionary is accompanied by legends, sayings, expressions, and stories.

LAFLESCHE, FRANCIS, Omaha.
The Middle Five: Indian Schoolboys of the Omaha Tribe. Madison: Univ. of Wisconsin Press, 1963. 152 pp. Illus. $1.65 paperbound.

This reprint of a 1900 edition describes LaFlesche's experiences at the Presbyterian Mission School, Bellevue, Nebraska, during the 1860's.

LAFLESCHE, FRANCIS, Omaha.
The Omaha Tribe, co-authored by Alice Cunningham Fletcher. Washington: Government Printing Office, 1911. 672 pp. Illus. Out of print.

The author describes the customs, ceremonies, and beliefs of the Omahas in the nineteenth century, before and after contact with whites.

LAFLESCHE, FRANCIS, Omaha.
The War Ceremony and Peace Ceremony of the Osage Indians. U.S. American Ethnology Bureau Bulletin 101. Washington: Government Printing Office, 1939. 280 pp. Out of print.

Songs and rituals are presented in English and Osage.

LEFT HANDED, Navajo.
Son of Old Man Hat: A Navajo Autobiography, as told to Walter Dyk. Lincoln: Univ. of Nebraska Press, 1967. 378 pp. $1.95 paperbound.

In this reprint of a 1938 edition, an old man recalls his first twenty years. Through an interpreter, he deals with such subjects as Navajo sex mores, family relationships, customs, and philosophy of life.

LONE DOG, LOUISE, Mohawk-Delaware.
Strange Journey: The Vision Quest of a Psychic Indian Woman. Healdsburg, Calif.: Naturegraph Co., 1964. $1.50 paperbound.

A psychic woman records her visions.

LONG, JAMES LARPENTEUR (FIRST BOY), Assiniboine.
The Assiniboines: From the Accounts of the Old Ones Told to First Boy, ed. and with an introduction by Michael Stephen Kennedy. Norman: Univ. of Oklahoma Press, 1961. 209 pp. Illus. $5.00.

Long interviewed and recorded twenty-five of the oldest members of the Assiniboine Tribe living in the 1930's. Their facts, stories, and recollections tell of the Assiniboine way of life.

LOWRY, ANNIE, Paiute.
Karnee: A Paiute Narrative, ed. by Lalla Scott. Reno: Univ. of Nevada Press, 1966. 149 pp. $5.25.

A Paiute woman who was born about 1860 narrates her life story, which includes a biography of her mother, Sau-tau-nee. Paiute history, legends, beliefs, customs, and encounters with whites are discussed.

MCNICKLE, D'ARCY, Flathead.
Indians and Other Americans, with Harold E. Fey.
New York: Harper and Row, 1959. 220 pp. Illus.
$3.75.

This comprehensive survey reviews the contacts between Indians and European colonists, wars, treaties, land deals, educative attempts, effects of relocation, urbanization, industrialization, and contemporary self-help programs designed to help Indians retain dignity and a sense of identity.

MCNICKLE, D'ARCY, Flathead.
The Indian Tribes of the United States: Ethnic and Cultural Survival. New York: Oxford Univ. Press, 1962. 79 pp. $1.75 paperbound.

Indian attempts to adjust to Anglo-American culture in contemporary American society are the subject of this work.

MCNICKLE, D'ARCY, Flathead.
The Surrounded. New York: Dodd, Mead, and Co., 1936. 297 pp. Out of print.

This novel about a tribe living on a reservation in western Montana focuses on the conflict between a boy's desire for a wider life and the traditions of his tribe.

MCNICKLE, D'ARCY, Flathead.
They Came Here First: The Epic of the American Indian. Philadelphia: J.B. Lippincott Co., 1949. 352 pp. Out of print.

Mr. McNickle traces the history of American Indians, from the first migrations to North America to their near-extinction under white domination.

MATHEWS, JOHN JOSEPH, Osage.
Life and Death of an Oilman: The Career of E.W. Marland. Norman: Univ. of Oklahoma Press, 1952. 259 pp. Illus. Out of print.

This biography of Marland (1874-1941) gives an account of his famous Oklahoma oil strikes and his dealings in high finance.

MATHEWS, JOHN JOSEPH, Osage.
The Osages: Children of the Middle Waters. Norman: Univ. of Oklahoma Press, 1961. 826 pp. Illus. $7.95.

This history of the Osage Tribe covers the periods before and after the coming of Europeans.

MATHEWS, JOHN JOSEPH, Osage.
Sundown. New York: Longmans, Green, and Co.,
1934. 312 pp. Out of print.

This is a novel about Chal Windzer, born about the turn of this century on the Osage Reservation in Oklahoma. Windzer goes to college, trains and serves as an aviator, and eventually returns to his own people after oil has been discovered on the tribal lands. The changes in Osage life and the destructive role of alien ideals and customs in Osage culture are treated in the novel.

MATHEWS, JOHN JOSEPH, Osage.
Talking to the Moon. Chicago: Univ. of Chicago
Press, 1945. 243 pp. Out of print.

Mathews presents the Osage interpretation for each of the twelve appearances of the moon, and the special significance for the earth of each such appearance.

MATHEWS, JOHN JOSEPH, Osage.
Wah'Kon-Tah: The Osage and the White Man's Road. Norman: Univ. of Oklahoma Press, 1932, 1968. 359 pp. Illus. $5.95.

A journal kept by Major Laban J. Miles, Osage agent from 1878 to 1931, provides the basis for this narrative. Mr. Mathews interprets the journal in light of his intimate knowledge of the tribe.

MITCHELL, EMERSON BLACKHORSE, Navajo.
Miracle Hill: The Story of a Navajo Boy, with T. D.
Allen. Norman: Univ. of Oklahoma Press, 1967.
230 pp. $5.95.

This is an autobiographical account of a young Navajo's life, from his birth in a hogan to his coming of age, from his relationships with his own family and environment to his dealings with the world of the white man.

MOMADAY, NATACHEE SCOTT, Kiowa.
House Made of Dawn. New York: Harper and Row,
1969. 224 pp. $4.95. Also paperbound: New York:
New American Library. $0.95.

This novel is about an ex-serviceman's relationship to two worlds—Indian and non-Indian—after World War II. He finds it difficult to fit into the white man's world or to go home to the Pueblo. Pulitzer Prize winner.

MOMADAY, NATACHEE SCOTT, Kiowa.
The Way to Rainy Mountain. Albuquerque: Univ. of
New Mexico Press, 1969. 89 pp. Illus. by A. M.
Momaday. $4.95. Also paperbound: New York:
Ballantine Books. $1.25.

Mr. Momaday retells the story of the migration of the Kiowas from the head-
waters of the Yellowstone River in what is now western Montana to Rainy
Mountain in the Southern Plains. The journey, begun three-hundred years ago, is
recalled in three voices: legendary, historical, and the author's contemporary
impressions.

MONTURE, ETHEL BRANT, Mohawk.
*Famous Indians: Brant, Crowfoot, and Oronhya-
tekha.* Toronto: Clarke, Irwin, and Co., Ltd., 1960.
160 pp. Illus. Cost unreported.

In this volume are the life stories of Brant (Mohawk), Crowfoot (Blackfeet)
and Oronhyatekha—or Peter Martin—(Mohawk).

MONTURE, ETHEL BRANT, Mohawk.
Joseph Brant, Mohawk, with Harvey Chalmers. East
Lansing, Mich.: Michigan State Univ. Press, 1955.
364 pp. $5.00.

This biography of Brant, an eighteenth century Mohawk, was written by one of
his descendants.

MONTURE, ETHEL BRANT, Mohawk.
West to the Setting Sun, with Harvey Chalmers. New
York: Macmillan Co., 1943. 362 pp. Out of print.

The career of Joseph Brant, in a book combining factual biography and historical
fiction, is treated against a background of military action. A picture emerges of a
people struggling to preserve their traditions and physical surroundings.

MORGAN, WILLIAM, Navajo.
Human-Wolves Among the Navajo. Yale Univ. Pub-
lications in Anthropology, No. 11. New Haven: Yale
Univ. Press, 1936. 43 pp. Out of print.

The author discusses the belief of the Navajos in human-wolves, men and women
disguised in wolf or mountain lion skin who practice witchcraft. He treats the
human-wolves as a variable in Navajo culture as a whole and tells the stories of
several Navajos who are concerned with this belief.

MORGAN, WILLIAM, Navajo.
Navajo-English Dictnonary, with Leon Wall. Window
Rock, Arizona: Navajo Agency, Branch of Educa-
tion, 1958. 65 pp. Out of print.

MORGAN, WILLIAM, Navajo.
Navajo Historical Selections, co-authored by Robert
W. Young. Lawrence, Kansas: Bureau of Indian
Affairs, 1954. 209 pp. $1.00 paperbound. Available
from Publications Service, Haskell Institute, Law-
rence, Kansas 66044.

A collection of stories and articles, written by Navajos, records events from the
past and also gives Navajo attitudes and reactions to historic events. Navajo and
English texts are provided.

MOUNTAIN WOLF WOMAN, Winnebago.
*Mountain Wolf Woman, Sister of Crashing Thunder:
The Autobiography of a Winnebago Woman,* ed. by
Nancy Oestreich Lurie. Ann Arbor: Univ. of Michi-
gan Press, 1961. 142 pp. $1.75 paperbound.

Mountain Wolf Woman, aged seventy-five, recorded everyday events of her past
life. This book is informative about Winnebago culture in Wisconsin and Nebraska.

MR. MOUSTACHE, Navajo.
*A Navajo Personal Document with a Brief Paretian
Analysis,* ed. by Clyde Kluckhohn, Southwestern
Journal of Anthropology, Vol. I. Albuquerque: Univ.
of New Mexico Press, 1945. pp. 260-283. Out of
print.

This brief life story of a Navajo born in 1868, told to Kluckhohn through an
interpreter, reveals ways in which social conditioning is carried on within the
tribe and contains data on the values of Navajo society.

MURIE, JAMES R., Pawnee.
Pawnee Indian Societies. Anthropological Papers of
the American Museum of Natural History, Vol. XI,
Part VII. New York: The Trustees, 1914. pp. 543-
644.

Discussions of Pawnee societies and a general outline of the tribal ceremonial
scheme are accompanied by descriptions of the place and significance of the
societies in Pawnee culture.

MURIE, JAMES R., Pawnee.
Traditions of the Skidi Pawnee, with George Amos
Dorsey. Memoirs of the American Folklore Society,
Vol. VIII. Boston: Houghton Mifflin and Co., 1904.
366 pp. Out of print.

Pawnee tales about tribal origins, rituals, medicine men, and encounters with
animals, are grouped here to convey the culture of the Pawnees.

NEQUATEWA, EDMUND, Hopi.
*Truth of a Hopi: Stories Relating to the Origin,
Myths, and Clan Histories of the Hopi.* Museum of
Northern Arizona Bulletin No. 8. Flagstaff: Arizona
Northland Press, 1967. 136 pp. $2.00 paperbound.

This reprint of a 1936 edition contains stories from Hopi tradition, myth, and
history. The sacred beliefs, wanderings, and trials of a group of Hopi clans are
also recounted.

NEWELL, WILLIAM B., Mohawk.
Crime and Justice Among the Iroquois. Montreal:
Caughnawaga Historical Society, 1965. 92 pp. Out
of print.

Iroquois society is briefly described here, with an analysis of social life, the relationship of crime to the society, specific crimes, punishments, and laws.

NEWLAND, SAM, and STEWART, JACK, Paiute.
Two Paiute Autobiographies, as told to Julian Haynes
Steward. Univ. of California Publications in Ameri-
can Archaeology and Ethnology, Vol. 33, No. 5.
Berkeley: Univ. of California Press, 1934. pp. 423-
438. Out of print.

Two men, both nearly one-hundred-years old but widely divergent in personality,
tell the stories of their lives and give insights into the dynamic aspects of Paiute
culture. Both men reached maturity before the coming of the white man to eastern
California in 1861.

NOWELL, CHARLES JAMES, Kwakiutl.
*Smoke from Their Fires: The Life of a Kwakiutl
Chief,* ed. by Chellan Stearns Ford. Hamden, Conn.:
Archon, 1968. 248 pp. Illus. $6.50.

Nowell, born in 1870, tells the story of his life commenting on Kwakiutl society
before and after contacts with whites. This is a reprint of a 1940 edition.

OLD MEXICAN, Navajo.
Old Mexican, A Navajo Autobiography, as told to
Walter Dyk. New York: Viking Fund Publications
in Anthropology, No. 8, 1947. 218 pp. Out of print.

This narrative of Old Mexican's life from 1871 (when he was five) to 1919 is
mainly about adult life in Navajo society.

ORTIZ, ALFONSO, San Juan Pueblo.
Project Head Start in an Indian Community. Chicago:
Univ. of Chicago Press, 1965. 70 pp. $3.60.

Dr. Ortiz discusses the influence of historical, social, and cultural factors upon
the early learning processes of San Juan Pueblo Indian children as related to the
conduct of Head Start Programs. Available from ERIC Document Reproduction
Service, NCR Co., 4936 Fairmont Ave., Bethesda, Md. 20014. Use the book's
reference number, ED 014 329.

ORTIZ, ALFONSO, San Juan Pueblo.
*The Tewa World: Space, Time, Being, and Becom-
ing in a Pueblo Society.* Chicago: Univ. of Chicago
Press, 1969. $8.00.

This analysis of the complex cosmological and ritual systems of the Tewa, an
eastern Pueblo society of the southwest U.S., is one of the most complete descriptions and interpretations ever published on the world view of an Indian tribe.

OSKISON, JOHN MILTON, Cherokee.
Brothers Three. New York: Macmillan Co., 1935.
448 pp. Out of print.

This novel, which starts in 1873, tells the story of an Oklahoma farm and the
family that owned it.

OSKISON, JOHN MILTON, Cherokee.
A Texas Titan: The Story of Sam Houston. Garden
City, N.Y.: Doubleday, Doran and Co., Inc., 1929.
311 pp. Out of print.

This story of Sam Houston's life includes his numerous contacts and friendships
with Indians.

OSKISON, JOHN MILTON, Cherokee.
*Tecumseh and His Times: The Story of a Great
Indian.* New York: G. P. Putnam's Sons, 1938. 244
pp. Out of print.

This is a biography of Tecumseh, a Shawnee, who struggled valiantly to protect Indian lands from white encroachment.

OWL, MRS. SAMSON et al. Catawba.
Catawba Texts, ed. by Frank G. Speck. Columbia Univ. Contributions to Anthropology Vol. XXIV. New York: Columbia Univ. Press, 1934. 91 pp. Out of print.

Catawba tales narrated by Mrs. Owl and several other members of the tribe through an interpreter are presented in Catawba and English texts (southeastern United States).

PARKER, ARTHUR CASWELL, Seneca.
A History of the Seneca Indians. Empire State Historical Publication No. 43. Port Washington, N.Y.: Friedman, 1967. 162 pp. $7.50.

Originally published in 1926, this book details the history and culture of the Senecas from their beginnings through the first quarter of the twentieth century.

PARKER, ARTHUR CASWELL, Seneca.
The Indian How Book. Garden City, N.Y.: Doubleday, Doran and Co., 1937. 355 pp. Out of print.

This book focuses on life in camp and on the trail.

PARKER, ARTHUR CASWELL, Seneca.
The Life of General Ely S. Parker: Last Grand Sachem of the Iroquois and General Grant's Military Secretary. Buffalo Historical Society Publications Vol. 23. Buffalo: Buffalo Historical Society, 1919. 346 pp. Out of print.

This narrative of the life of E. S. Parker, who was born in 1828, by his great-nephew, includes material on the home life, social status, and relationships of a Seneca family.

PARKER, ARTHUR CASWELL, Seneca.
Parker on the Iroquois. Syracuse, N.Y.: Syracuse Univ. Press, 1968. Pages unreported. $8.95.

A compilation of early twentieth century works, this book includes "Iroquois Uses of Maize and Other Food Plants," "The Code of Handsome Lake, the Seneca Prophet," and "The Constitution of the Five Nations."

PARKER, ARTHUR CASWELL, Seneca.
Red Jacket: Last of the Senecas. New York: Mc-
Graw-Hill, 1952. 288 pp. Illus. Out of print.

This history of Red Jacket, a Seneca born in 1750, includes narrative material
expressing his preference for the Seneca way of life, and details his efforts to
protect the Senecas from the encroachments of an alien civilization.

PARKER, ARTHUR CASWELL, Seneca.
Seneca Myths and Folk Tales. Buffalo Historical So-
ciety Publications Vol. 27. Buffalo: Buffalo Historical
Society, 1923. 465 pp. Illus. Out of print.

This collection of oral literature from the Senecas of western New York includes
myths, legends, fiction, and traditions that reveal Seneca customs, interests and
daily life.

PARRISH, ESSIE, see HERMAN, JAMES et al.,
Kashaya.

PHINNEY, ARCHIE, Nez Perce.
Nez Perce Texts. Columbia Univ. Contributions to
Anthropology Vol. XXV. New York: Columbia
Univ. Press, 1934. 497 pp. Out of print.

A collection of ancient Nez Perce tales narrated to the author by his sixty-year-old
mother, Wayilatpu. Nez Perce and English texts are provided.

PLENTY-COUPS, Crow.
Plenty-Coups, Chief of the Crows, ed. by Frank
Bird Linderman. Lincoln: Univ. of Nebraska Press,
1962. 324 pp. $1.50 paperbound.

Eighty-year-old Chief Plenty-Coups discusses his boyhood, how he became chief,
and how he participated in the tribal customs of the Crow Indians. This book was
originally published in 1930 as *American, The Life Story of a Great Indian,
Plenty-Coups, Chief of the Crows.*

QOYAWAYMA, POLINGAYSI
(ELIZABETH Q. WHITE), Hopi.
*No Turning Back: A True Account of a Hopi Indian
Girl's Struggle to Bridge the Gap Between the World
of Her People and the World of the White Man,* as
told to Vada F. Carlson. Albuquerque: Univ. of New
Mexico Press, 1964. 180 pp. $5.00.

This narrative of a Hopi woman, born about 1892, who chooses in her early
youth to live in the white man's world also includes information on Hopi legend,
ceremony, religion, and philosophy.

RED HORSE OWNER, Sioux.
*Red Horse Owner's Winter Count: The Oglala
Sioux 1786-1968,* ed. by Joseph S. Karol. Martin,
S. Dak.: The Booster Publishing Co., 1969. 68 pp.
Illus. $1.50 paperbound. Available from Tipi Shop,
Inc., P.O. Box 1270, Rapid City, South Dakota
57701.

The Sioux Winter Count is a calendric chronological recorded history and contains a yearly pictographic symbol (explained in the accompanying text) representing the people, places, or events that made each year notable.

RIDGE, JOHN ROLLIN (YELLOW BIRD),
Cherokee.
*The Life and Adventures of Joaquin Murieta, the
Celebrated California Bandit.* Norman: Univ. of
Oklahoma Press, 1962. 159 pp. Illus. $2.95.

This biography of Murieta describes the life and career of California's most legendary bandit.

RIDGE, JOHN ROLLIN (YELLOW BIRD),
Cherokee.
Poems. San Francisco: Henry Payot and Co., Publishers, 1868. 137 pp. Out of print.

This book of poems primarily about nature and women includes an autobiographical sketch.

SEKAQUAPTEWA, HELEN, Hopi.
Me and Mine: The Life Story of Helen Sekaquaptewa, as told to Louise Udall. Tucson: Univ. of
Arizona Press, 1969. 262 pp. $3.95 paperbound.

This autobiographical narrative describes the way a Hopi woman was able to build a rewarding life by combining the best that the white and Hopi worlds have to offer.

SENUNGETUK, JOSEPH, Eskimo.
*Give or Take a Century: The Story of an Eskimo
Family.* San Francisco: The Indian Historian Press,
1970. 120 pp. Illus. by author. $6.00.

The author tells the history of an Eskimo family in Alaska as they moved from a century which was filled with the customs, traditions, and life ways of an ancient time into a new century in which the people are confronted and confused by the mores, social life, and technology of a different culture.

SEWID, JAMES, Kwakiutl.
Guests Never Leave Hungry: The Autobiography of James Sewid, A Kwakiutl Indian, ed. by James P. Spradley. New Haven: Yale Univ. Press, 1969. 310 pp. $10.00.

Sewid, an hereditary chief, tells the story of his life and the organizational and civic concerns of a growing Kwakiutl settlement.

SHAW, ANNA MOORE, Pima.
Pima Indian Legends. Tucson: Univ. of Arizona Press, 1968. 111 pp. $2.50 paperbound.

Mrs. Shaw relates stories heard from her parents and grandparents, and combines ancient Pima history with more current happenings.

SON OF FORMER MANY BEADS, Navajo.
The Ramah Navajos, ed. by Robert W. Young and William Morgan. Lawrence, Kansas: Bureau of Indian Affairs, 1967. 17 pp. 10¢ paperbound. Available from Publications Service, Haskell Institute, Lawrence, Kansas 66044.

This booklet is one of a series of bilingual brochures. It deals with matters of hisorical significance to the Navajo, and discusses the development of the land problems of the Navajo in the Ramah (New Mexico) area.

STANDING BEAR, LUTHER, Sioux.
Land of the Spotted Eagle. Boston: Houghton Mifflin Co., 1933. 259 pp. Illus. Out of print.

Chief Standing Bear describes his early life and the manners, customs, morals, and characteristics of his people.

STANDING BEAR, LUTHER, Sioux.
My Indian Boyhood. Boston: Houghton Mifflin Co., York: Houghton Mifflin Co., 1928. 288 pp. Illus. Out of print.

A Sioux chief, who was a member of the first class at Carlisle, tells of his home, school and reservation life, his marriage, and work for the advancement of the tribe.

STANDING BEAR, LUTHER, Sioux.
My People, The Sioux, ed. by E.A. Brininstool. New 1931. 189 pp. Illus. Out of print.

Chief Standing Bear relates memories of his boyhood, giving a great deal of information about the Sioux tribe and how their chiefs are made.

STANDS IN TIMBER, JOHN, Cheyenne.
Cheyenne Memories, A Folk History, with Margot
Liberty and Robert M. Utley. New Haven: Yale
Univ. Press, 1967. 330 pp. Illus. $7.95.

Stands In Timber has narrated a wide range of Cheyenne experience, from legendary times to life on the Northern Cheyenne Reservation in Montana. *Cheyenne Memories* represents his personal effort to preserve the history of his people.

STEWART, JACK, see NEWLAND, SAM, Paiute.

SWEEZY, CARL, Arapaho.
The Arapaho Way: A Memoir of an Indian Boyhood,
as told to Althea Bass. New York: Clarkson N.
Potter, Inc., 1966. 88 pp. Illus. by author. $5.95.

Mr. Sweezy, born in 1881, relates his memories of Arapaho culture's "old ways." His illustrations depict dances, hunts, games, dress, and ceremonies.

TALAYESVA, DON C., Hopi.
Sun Chief: The Autobiography of a Hopi Indian, ed.
by Leo W. Simmons. New Haven: Yale Univ. Press,
1942. 460 pp. $2.95 paperbound.

This frank autobiography describes Talayesva's first ten years (1890-1900) in the Hopi village of Oraibi, Arizona, and then the subsequent decade spent in schools in Arizona and California.

TOWENDOLLY, GRANT, Wintu.
A Bag of Bones, ed. by Marcelle Masson. Healdsburg, Calif.: Naturegraph Publishers, date and pages
unreported. $1.95 paperbound.

Stories and legends of the Wintu Indians of northern California are told by a member of the tribe.

TWO LEGGINGS, Crow.
Two Leggings: The Making of a Crow Warrior, ed.
by Peter Nabokov. New York: Thomas Y. Crowell,
1967. 226 pp. $6.95.

This first-person account of the everyday life of a nineteenth-century Crow Indian man provides a primary source for understanding, and witnessing in action, the religious and social values of a Plains Indian people.

VAUDRIN, BILL, Chippewa.
Tanaina Tales from Alaska. Norman: Univ. of Oklahoma Press, 1969. Pages unreported. $4.95.

The author, who has lived and taught in Alaska for years, has gathered a collection of stories handed down through the generations.

VELARDE, PABLITA, Santa Clara Pueblo.
Old Father, The Story Teller. Globe, Ariz.: Dale Stuart King, 1960. 66 pp. Illus. by author. $7.95.

An Indian painter writes the stories and legends she heard from her grandfather and great-grandfather.

VILLASENOR, DAVID, Otomi.
Tapestries in Sand: The Spirit of Indian Sandpainting. Healdsburg, Calif.: Naturegraph Publishers, date unreported. 112 pp. Illus. $2.95 paperbound.

The author, who has learned sandpainting from Navajo medicine men, writes about this ancient art and its meanings.

WEBB, GEORGE, Pima.
A Pima Remembers. Tucson: Univ. of Arizona Press, 1959. 126 pp. Illus. $3.00.

Mr. Webb relates Pima history and traditions in the form of short stories. The book is designed both to acquaint young Pima readers with their own traditions and to familiarize white readers with the position of Pimas in modern American life.

WELCH, JAMES, Blackfeet.
Young American Poets, by P. Carroll. Chicago: Big Table Publishing Company, 1968. Pages unreported. $4.95 paperbound.

Nine poems by Mr. Welch about reservation life are included in this collection of poetry by young Americans.

WHITE BULL, JOSEPH, Sioux.
The Warrior Who Killed Custer: The Personal Narrative of Chief Joseph White Bull, trans. and ed. by James H. Howard. Lincoln: Univ. of Nebraska Press, 1969. 84 pp. Illus. by author. $6.95.

Writing in Dakota (Sioux) and using traditional pictographs, Chief White Bull describes hunts and battles in which he participated, including three accounts of the killing of Custer. Also included is a traditional winter count of the western Sioux, covering the years from 1764 to 1931.

WHITEWOLF, JIM, Kiowa Apache.
Jim Whitewolf: The Life of a Kiowa Apache Indian,
ed. by Charles S. Brant. New York: Dover Books,
1969. 144 pp. $1.75.

This life story of a Kiowa Apache born in the second half of the nineteenth century
was dictated in 1949 and 1950 and describes tribal society under white influence.

WILLOYA, WILLIAM, Eskimo.
Warriors of the Rainbow, co-authored by Vinson
Brown. Healdsburg, Calif.: Naturegraph Publishers,
date unreported. 104 pp. Illus. $2.25 paperbound.

A study of Indian dreams is accompanied by full-color reproductions of paintings
done by Indian artists. An appendix gives the scientific basis for the study.

WINNIE, LUCILLE "JERRY"
(SAH-GAN-DE-OH), Seneca-Cayuga.
Sah-gan-de-oh, the Chief's Daughter. New York:
Vantage Press, 1968. 190 pp. $3.95.

This is an autobiography of a twentieth century Seneca-Cayuga woman who grew
up on reservations in Oklahoma, Montana, and Kansas.

WOODEN LEG, Cheyenne.
Wooden Leg: A Warrior Who Fought Custer, as told
to Thomas B. Marquis. Lincoln: Univ. of Nebraska
Press, 1962. 389 pp. $1.90 paperbound.

This reprint of a 1931 edition is the narrative of a Cheyenne warrior who fought
against Custer at the Battle of the Little Big Horn. It includes observations on
Cheyenne daily life and tribal customs.

WORKING INDIANS CIVIL ASSOCIATION,
Dakota Sioux.
A Dakota-English Dictionary. Pierre, S. Dak.: Work-
ing Indians Civil Association, 1969. Pages unreported.
$6.00.

The purpose of this book is to impart an appreciation of Siouan heritage and
culture through a study of Dakota. The book may be obtained from W.I.C.A.,
Box 537, Pierre, S. Dak.

WRIGHT, MURIEL HAZEL, Choctaw.
A Guide to the Indian Tribes of Oklahoma. Norman:
Univ. of Oklahoma Press, 1965. 300 pp. Illus. $5.95.

Brief histories of sixty-five tribes either indigenous to Oklahoma or relocated there by the Federal government are augmented by a summary of the role played by Indians in the evolution of the Oklahoma area.

WRIGHT, MURIEL HAZEL. Choctaw.
Oklahoma: A History of the State and Its People,
with Joseph B. Thoburn. New York: Lewis Historical
Publishing Co., Inc., 1929. 4 vols. Out of print.

Volumes I and II of this work cover Oklahoma history from ancient times to the 1920's. Volumes III and IV contain the biographies of prominent Oklahomans.

WRIGHT, MURIEL HAZEL, Choctaw.
Springplace: Moravian Mission and the Ward Family
of the Cherokee Nation. Guthrie, Okla.: Co-operative
Publishing Co., 1940. 93 pp. Illus. Out of print.

This volume presents a brief outline of the development of the Cherokee Nation and traces the role of Christianity in the Nation's history.

YELLOW ROBE, ROSEBUD (LACOTAWIN),
Sioux.
An Album of the American Indian. New York:
Franklin Watts, Inc., 1969. 96 pp. Illus. $3.95.

Paintings, drawings, and photographs, accompanied by a brief text, serve to illustrate various facets of American Indian cultures and history from past to present. Although designed primarily for young adults, this album will be of interest to all ages.

YELLOW WOLF, Nez Perce.
The Last Stand of the Nez Perce: Destruction of a
People, with Harvey Chalmers II. New York:
Twayne Publishers, 1962. 288 pp. Illus. Out of
Print.

Chalmers gives a narrative account, based on recorded history, of the events leading to war between the Nez Perce and the United States Army in 1877. Then Yellow Wolf, a nephew of Chief Joseph, gives an account of the same events, told through an interpreter.

YOUNG, LUCY, Wailaki.
"Out of the Past: A True Indian Story," as told to
Edith V.A. Murray in the *California Historical
Society Quarterly* Vol. XX, No. 4. Dec. 1941. pp.
349-364. Out of print.

These memoirs were dictated in 1939 by a ninety-year-old woman who recalled
her childhood and the occurrences of everyday life. The major part of the narrative takes place in 1862.

MISCELLANEOUS

ARCHIQUETTE, OSCAR, Oneida.
Oneida Indians of Wisconsin Hymn Book, compiled
by Oscar Archiquette. Oneida, Wisc.: Oscar Archiquette, 1965. Unpaged. $5.00.

The hymns in this volume are printed in Oneida.

The National Indian Youth Council plans to publish in 1970 a collection of the
speeches and writings of the late Clyde Warrior, a founder of NIYC and an
outspoken militant. For information write to: National Indian Youth Council,
3102 Central S. E., Albuquerque, N.M. 87106

ASTROV, MARGOT.
American Indian Prose and Poetry: An Anthology. New York: Capricorn Books, 1962. 366 pp. $1.45 paperbound.

Two introductory chapters by the author are followed by translated North, Central, and South American Indian songs, speeches, prayers, myths, and personal narratives.

CLARK, ELLA ELIZABETH.
Indian Legends of Canada. Toronto: McClelland and Stewart, 1960. 177 pp. $4.50.

This anthology contains oral literature from thirty tribes, based on legends, myths, personal narratives, and historical tradition.

CURTIS, NATALIE.
The Indians' Book: Songs and Legends of the American Indians. New York: Dover Publications, Inc., 1969. 584 pp. Illus. $4.00 paperbound.

Reprinted from a 1907 edition, this is a collection of traditional music and songs of eighteen tribes, and includes drawings, legends, photographs, and stories.

DAY, A. GROVE.
The Sky Clears: Poetry of the American Indian. Lincoln: University of Nebraska, 1964. 204 pp. $1.75 paperbound.

This book brings together more than two hundreds poems and lyrics from about forty North American tribes.

FORBES, JACK D.
"Voices from Native America," in *The Indian In America's Past.* Englewood Cliffs, N.J.: Prentice-Hall, 1964. pp. 54-73. $1.95 paperbound.

Excerpts from speeches and statements by American Indians, covering the period from 1609 to 1963, touch on a wide range of subjects.

HAMILTON, CHARLES EVERETT.
Cry of the Thunderbird: The American Indian's Own Story. New York: Macmillan, 1950. 283 pp. Illus. Out of print.

Illustrated entirely by Indian artists, this collection includes about 100 stories and speeches written or dictated by North American Indians.

JONES, LOUIS THOMAS.
Aboriginal American Oratory. Los Angeles: Southwest Museum, 1965. 136 pp. Illus. $5.00.

Collected speeches from Indian orators are supplemented with historical explanations and discussions of American Indian language forms.

MALLERY, GARRICK.
Picture-Writing of the American Indians. American Ethnology Bureau Annual Report, Vol. 10, 1888-1889. Washington: Government Printing Office, 1893. 822 pp. Illus.

Anonymous pictographers are primarily the authors of this treatise on Canadian, North, Central, and South American Indian picture-writing. Profusely illustrated chapters include pictography relating to chronology, totems, religion, customs, history, biography, ideology, and the significance of colors.

MARRIOTT, ALICE, and RACHLIN, CAROL
American Indian Mythology. New York: Thomas Y. Crowell Co., 1968. 211 pp. Illus. $7.95.

The myths, legends, and contemporary folklore of some twenty North American tribes are presented in this collection.

SOUTH DAKOTA REVIEW.
"Poetry, Fiction, Art, Music, Religion by The American Indian", in the *South Dakota Review,* Vol. 7, No. 2. Vermillion, S. Dak.: University of South Dakota Press, 1969. 194 pp. Illus. $1.50.

This collection of writing and painting represents tribal groups primarily from the western half of the country.

THOMPSON, STITH.
Tales of the North American Indians. Bloomington: Indiana University Press, 1966. 386 pp. $2.95 paperbound.

This collection of tales from numerous tribes is arranged by story content rather than by tribe or area. The arrangement is in accord with the compiler's theory that there are many recurrent patterns or types of tales which transcend geographic and linguistic boundaries.

SUPPLEMENT II: PERIODIC PUBLICATIONS

AKWESASNE NOTES, c/o Jerry Gambill, Box 435, Rooseveltown, N.Y. 13683. No subscription rate quoted. Published monthly.

The paper is assembled at Akwesasne, also known as the St. Regis Mohawk Reserve, by White Roots of Peace, an Indian communications unit. A collection of articles reproduced from Indian and non-Indian press covering varied aspects of contemporary Indian affairs.

THE CHEROKEE ONE FEATHER, P.O. Box 501, Cherokee, N.C. 28719. Annual subscription: $5.00. Published weekly.

Sponsored by the tribal council of the Eastern Band of Cherokees, this paper is devoted to reporting council action, community happenings, and inter-tribal news.

CITY SMOKE SIGNALS, 114 West 6th St., Sioux City, Ia. 51103. No subscription rate quoted. Published monthly.

This mimeographed newspaper is published by the Sioux City American Indian Center to inform the Indian people of the Sioux City metropolitan area about programs, services, and social activities available to them through the Center, as well as informing non-Indians about Indian affairs.

EARLY AMERICAN, 708 Mills Ave., Modesto, Calif. 95350. Annual subscription: $3.00. Published every two months.

This newsletter of the California Indian Education Association contains information on Indian education and related matters as well as news of other Indian groups, books about Indians, achievements of Indian people and editorial comment.

FORT APACHE SCOUT, P.O. Box 898, Whiteriver, Ariz. 85941. Annual subscription: $1.50. Published monthly.

The official newspaper of the White Mountain Apache Tribe carries tribal news.

INDIAN AFFAIRS IN CALIFORNIA, P.O. Box 389, Sacramento, Calif. 95802. For subscription rates and publishing schedule, write to publication.

This publication of the California League for American Indians contains California Indian news as well as national Indian news.

INDIAN-ESKIMO ASSOCIATION OF CANADA BULLETIN, 277 Victoria St., Toronto 200, Ontario, Canada. For subscription rates and publishing schedule write: Mrs. Edith Fowke, Editor.

The publication of the Indian-Eskimo Association of Canada contains news of Indian affairs in Canada.

THE INDIAN HISTORIAN, 1451 Masonic Ave., San Francisco, Calif. 94117. Annual subscription: $5.00. Published quarterly.

This journal published by the American Indian Historical Society carries scholarly articles by Indians and non-Indians covering a wide range of subjects, historical and contemporary, including Indian cultures, philosophies, languages, art and education. Books about Indians are reviewed.

JICARILLA CHIEFTAIN, P.O. Box 147, Dulce, N.M. 87528. Annual subscription: $2.00. Published twice a month.

Published by the Jicarilla Apache Tribe, this paper contains tribal, community, and state news regarding Indians.

MANY SMOKES: NATIONAL INDIAN MAGAZINE, P.O. Box 5895, Reno, Nev. 89503. Annual subscription: $2.00. Published monthly.

This journal carries current national Indian news along with historical articles, legends and book reviews written by American Indians.

THE NATIVE NEVADAN, 1995 East 2nd St., Reno, Nev. 89502. Annual subscription: $2.50. Published monthly.

The official newspaper of the Inter-Tribal Council of Nevada, Inc. (Paiute, Shoshone, Washoe) publishes news of the Indian tribes and colonies in Nevada, as well as some national news.

THE NCAI SENTINEL, 1346 Connecticut Ave., N.W., Washington, D.C. 20036. Annual subscription: $3.00. Published quarterly.
The journal of the National Congress of American Indians carries national news pertaining to all Indian tribes and reservations.

THE NAVAJO TIMES, P.O. Box 428, Window Rock, Ariz. 86515. Annual subscription: $5.00. Published weekly.

This newspaper is owned by and intended primarily for the Navajo Tribe, but carries some news of other tribes and Indian communities.

PAPAGO INDIAN NEWS, Sells, Ariz. 85634. Annual subscription: $1.00. Published monthly.

This mimeographed paper carries tribal news, opinion, and news of individuals and families.

ROSEBUD SIOUX HERALD (EYAPAHA), Box 65, Rosebud, S. Dak. 57570. Annual subscription: $9.00. Published weekly.

Published for and owned by the Rosebud Sioux Tribe, this paper carries tribal news, some national news, and includes *The Woyakapi,* a student newspaper from St. Francis High School in St. Francis, S. Dak.

SMOKE SIGNALS, Parker, Ariz. 85344. For subscription rates and publishing schedule write to publication.

This mimeographed newspaper, the official tribal publication of the Mohave and Chemehuevi Tribes, contains ordinances, tribal council actions, correspondence and news.

SOUTHERN UTE DRUM, Tribal Affairs Bldg., Ignacio, Colo. 81137. Annual subscription: $4.00. Published every two weeks.

Published by the Southern Ute Tribe, this paper reports tribal news and community activities.

TALKING LEAVES, 3446 West First St., Los Angeles, Calif. 90004. Annual subscription: $2.50. Published monthly.

This publication of the Los Angeles Indian Center carries current national and Los Angeles area Indian news as well as historical articles and book reviews.

TUNDRA TIMES, Box 1287, Fairbanks, Alaska 99701. Annual subscription: $8.00 regular mail, $19.00 air mail. Published weekly.

Owned and controlled by the Eskimo, Indian and Aleut Publishing Company, a corporation of Alaska Natives, this newspaper prints information about Native concerns and events.

THE WARPATH, P.O. Box 26149, San Francisco, Calif. 94126. Annual subscription: $5.00 for non-Indians, $3.00 for Indians.

This publication of the United Native Americans, Inc. includes information on current Indian movements and organizations in America and Canada.

THE WARRIOR, 1630 West Wilson Ave., Chicago, Ill. 60640. Annual subscription: $2.50. Published ten times a year.

This journal published by the American Indian Center of Chicago contains news about the Center and Indians living in the Chicago area.

American Indian Calendar 1970. $3.00. Available from
American Indian Calendar, P.O. Box 18421, Capitol Hill
Station, Denver, Colorado 80218.

This year's calendar is illustrated with contemporary basketry created by tribal craftsmen across the United States. Descriptions of important events in Indian history accompany the appropriate date in each month. Quotations from speeches by Indians are also included.